Abingdon
MANUAL of
INSTALLATION
SERVICES

E. JANE MALL

Abingdon Press

Nashville

Abingdon Manual of Installation Services

Copyright © 1983 by Abingdon Press

Second Printing 1983

Library of Congress Cataloging in Publication Data

MALL, E. JANE, 1920-
   Abingdon manual of installation services.
   1. Installation service (Church officers) I. Title.
   BV199.I5M34   1983   265'.9   82-11438

ISBN 0-687-00367-9

MANUFACTURED BY THE PARTHENON PRESS AT
NASHVILLE, TENNESSEE, UNITED STATES OF AMERICA

Abingdon
Manual of
Installation
Services

Praise ye the Lord.
Praise God in his sanctuary:
praise him in the firmament
of his power.
Praise him for his mighty acts;
praise him according to his
excellent greatness.
Praise him with the sound
of the trumpet:
praise him with the psaltery
and harp.
Praise him with the timbrel and dance:
praise him with stringed instruments and
organs.
Praise him upon the loud cymbals:
praise him upon the high sounding
cymbals.
Let every thing that hath breath praise the
Lord. Praise ye the Lord.

(Psalm 150 KJV)

A FEW WORDS
FROM THE AUTHOR

A pastor I know came to me not long ago. "We have an installation coming up and I can't find an appropriate installation service. Do you know of any?" Because I love this particular young pastor a lot, I was willing to search some book stores and libraries to try to find the installation service he was looking for.

My search proved fruitless, and when I told him so, he was not surprised. "I guess I'll just have to write my own," he said.

That gave me an idea. How many pastors, I wondered, had written their own installation services? I talked to several pastors, and all of them admitted that they had written their own. "I've got my notes somewhere in my files," or, "I think the church secretary kept the program for one I wrote." This book is the result of my asking for permission to share some of these original installation services.

There is no reason why new liturgies shouldn't be used. Who says that these ceremonies (or celebrations, or acts of installation) must be uniform; or that, heaven forbid, the same old ones that have been used for generations must be used "because that's what we have always done!" I hope that this book is only a springboard to creativity for many of our clergy, and that they will use some of the services and will also see opportunities to change them, rework them to their own purposes; and even be inspired to write their own. This book is designed not as a book to use as is, but as a workbook.

An installation service is simply an act of publicly installing a person into the ministry or some special office in the church. The action is pretty much the same in all installation services, and they can be very elaborate or quite simple. The use of words, how thoughts are expressed, is what really makes an installation service unique.

Most installation services follow this general pattern:

1. An introduction and announcement of the purpose of the service.
2. A statement about the services that are to be performed by the person(s) being installed, and the reading of Scripture verses relevant to these services or duties.
3. The person being installed is asked to promise to faithfully perform certain duties.
4. The person(s) is given the congregation's trust and promise of cooperation.
5. All ask for God's blessing.

This is a simple outline, but it includes the basic steps of an installation service. Prayers, hymns, processionals, recessionals, special choir music, and so forth can be added to the service at the appropriate places.

This book can and should serve a dual purpose: you can use the services as they appear in the book, with minor changes, but you can also adapt some of them to fit different situations and different needs. For example, the service for a graduation can be adapted for use when a pastor is leaving the congregation, when a family is moving away, when a staff member is resigning, or for any other important leavetaking.

I have tried to cover all the possibilities, and there is at least one sample of each kind of installation. However, you may like the words of admonition in one service, the prayer in another, and the Scripture verses in still another. So put them together and write your own installation service. Change words, include the name of the church and names of the participants, and include personal items, so that you have a truly personalized installation service. In this way, this book should serve as a basis for installation services for many years to come.

Most of our installation services have evolved from certain customs and forms that have come down to us from experimentation. The important thing to remember is that it is the office or ministry that is important, not the ritual. The participants and the congregation should be able to understand the meaning of the service and its importance, regardless of how it is done.

We can do away with high-sounding mumbo-jumbo and rituals that have become almost meaningless, by using fresh, new forms and words that make the people sit up and listen to what is being said. An installation service should never be a performance in which the congregation sits back and watches a few people perform a rite. The people being installed should never need to ask afterward, "Just what went on? What was really said?" An installation service must be participatory, with everyone sharing in the service and the resulting obligations and ministry. Names should be named.

"Do you, John _____, promise . . ." rather than, "Do you, our brother in Christ, promise. . . ."

Free yourself to use new installation services, to show the people that what is going on is important and that it is personal. Get them involved. Use candles, banners, music, anything that will help them to know that this is something they are doing, not some rite being performed for them. In some instances, just having the congregation applaud at an appropriate point in the service is a way of involving them. The main thing to remember when planning an installation service is that what you do is not as important as why you are doing it.

E. Jane Mall

ACKNOWLEDGMENTS

I sent out a call for original and adapted installation services and the response was heartwarming. Thank you, from the bottom of my heart, and with love, to the following pastors who contributed to this book.

The Reverend Dwain Acker
Regional Minister
First Christian Church
Omaha, Nebraska 68152

The Reverend Gary S.
  Anderson
Valley of Peace Lutheran
  Church
4735 Bassett Creek Dr.
Golden Valley, Minnesota
  55422

Dr. Edward W. Bergstraesser
Senior Minister
First United Church
Oak Park, Illinois 60302

Paul R. Brinkman, Pastor
Faith Lutheran Church
1900 North Union
Appleton, Wisconsin 54911

The Reverend Wayne H.
  Carlson
St. Luke's Episcopal Church
1101 Sulphur Springs Road
Manchester, Missouri 63011

The Reverend R. Boyd Carter
First Congregational Church
P.O. Box 333
Terre Haute, Indiana 47807

The Reverend Winburn C.
  Davis

Southside Baptist Church
2420 Norfolk Street
Augusta, Georgia 30906

The Reverend Kenneth F.
  Frankenstein
Trinity Lutheran Church
1960 E. Johns Ave.
Decatur, Illinois 62521

The Reverend Paul Guffin
First United Methodist
  Church
1002 Eleventh Ave.
Delano, California 93215

The Reverend Scott C. Hall
Altoona United Methodist
  Church
602 5th Ave. SW
Altoona, Iowa 50009

Lorman M. Petersen, Pastor
Faith Lutheran Church
1900 North Union
Appleton, Wisconsin 54911

The Reverend David L.
  Schrader
Trinity Lutheran Church
1960 E. Johns Ave.
Decatur, Illinois 62521

The Reverend Philip C. Tesch
Trinity Lutheran Church

1960 E. Johns Ave.
Decatur, Illinois 62521

The Reverend Gary

Wollersheim
Hosanna! Lutheran Church
1819 Indiana St.
St. Charles, Illinois 60174

AND . . . To those pastors in several states and of several denominations who so generously contributed to this book, but preferred not to have their names mentioned, thank you!

CONTENTS

PLANNING
THE INSTALLATION SERVICE

■ Think about the physical facilities: whether or not you will have a processional march at the beginning of the service and who will participate in it.

■ An installation service does not always have to be in the sanctuary, on a Sunday morning or during an evening service. It would be just as "official" if held on a week night, or in the afternoon. It could be held in the parish hall, at a member's home, in a park, at the beach, or on the church lawn.

■ The entire service sould be carefully planned in every detail. Take time to choose appropriate hymns and special music. Use the talents of people in the congregation. Talk to all who will be participating to be sure they perfectly understand their part.

■ Consider special effects: lighting, banners, vocal numbers, instruments.

■ For the benediction, consider having certain members of the congregation participate from their places in the congregation, with responses, prayers, and so on. The benediction could be divided into several statements, spoken by members situated at strategic places throughout the congregation.

■ None of the services in this book is long enough for a morning or evening service. They are all designed to fit into a regular service of worship. However, any of them can be lengthened, particularly by the addition of a sermon or message by the pastor or someone else. You will have to supply the hymns and special music.

■ You could use the releasing of a quantity of balloons as a symbolic gesture of joy, the Holy Spirit, or unity.

■ You could have someone carry a blank flannel banner in the processional. During the service, different people add a symbolic piece to the banner, and then the completed banner is carried in the recessional.

■ A certain number of participants could hold up pieces of colored cardboard that, when put together, would form a large rainbow symbolic of hope and faith and promise.

In all of these installation services there are admonitions and statements of affirmation and confirmation; and they contain some very good thoughts. During the service, these words are spoken, but there is no time for reflection. It would be an excellent idea to have the programs printed well in advance and have an adult study class use these words for deep study.

For example, the members of the congregation are asked if they will support the pastor, and several ways of doing so are mentioned. The class could study these one by one, enlarging on them, using the appropriate Scripture verses, stating definite ways in which they will try to keep these promises and commitments. This would be a very good basis for an in-depth study and would certainly make the

installation service more meaningful to those who
had attended the class.

Some of the printed installation services have
beautiful covers, some with art work done by a
member of the congregation. Most of them list the
names of the participants along with a brief
biography of each. A few have a page of "Service
Notes," something like this:

> In Jesus' name we welcome each other to this celebration of
> our service of installation for Pastor _____. Members of this
> church greet especially you who share in our festive worship
> as guests.
>
> May the Holy Spirit of God use this celebration to come to
> us all in abundant measure. And when the service is finished
> may we all go forth with renewed zeal in continuing service to
> our gracious Lord.
>
> Officiants for this celebration are: *(here all are listed with a
> brief biography of each)*.
>
> Much gratitude needs to be expressed to many members of
> this congregation who in numerous ways are helping to make
> this celebration more festive and meaningful. We think
> particularly of: *(here are listed all those who have helped and a
> brief description of what they did)*.
>
> Our thoughts are thankful for the men and women who
> joined forces in painting the parsonage in preparation for the
> arrival of the new pastor. Members of the custodial and
> secretarial staff have gladly devoted extra energies to this
> occasion. So, to all of you, to everybody involved in any way,
> and in the name of the Lord Jesus Christ, for whom, finally
> and most of all, it is done: thank you in his name!

You will note that there is no special service of
ordination/installation of a woman pastor. I prayed
about this! I do not believe it is necessary to have a
special service for the ordination or installation of a
woman pastor. After all, a pastor is a pastor is a
pastor. Use the regular installation or ordination
services and simply change *he* to *she, him* to *her.*

THE LAYING ON OF HANDS: Numbers 27:18-19 KJV: "And the Lord said to Moses, Take thee Joshua the son of Nun, a man in whom is the spirit, and lay thine hand upon him; And set him before Eleazar the priest, and before all the congregation; and give him a charge in their sight."

In any ordination/installation service the laying on of hands may be used. There is nothing "mysterious" about it, it is simply an outward gesture of blessing. Also, there is no reason why the laying on of hands couldn't be used in any installation service, not only for the ordination of a pastor. In some instances, former or outgoing officers could lay hands on the new, incoming officers. In other cases, perhaps certain members of the congregation could come forward and lay hands on the candidates.

GENERAL FORMAT OF AN INSTALLATION SERVICE

Following is a general format that may be followed in planning an installation service. If this is used, it would probably be incorporated into a regular worship service. However, any part or parts of it can be lifted and used as desired.

Prelude
Processional
Hymn of welcome
Introit (Scripture verse(s))

The Gloria Patri
The Collect
The Epistle Lesson (Scripture)
Choir anthem
The Gospel Lesson (Scripture)
The Apostle's Creed
Hymn
The message from God's Word (sermon)
Offering
The Rite of Installation: Charge to the Candidate
                          Response
                          Charge to the
                             Congregation
                          Response
                          Prayer
The Lord's Prayer
Recessional
Benediction
Postlude

Somewhere on the printed bulletin, or in an insert, all officiants are listed. In the case of an ordination and installation of a pastor, the pastor's biography is included. Often, an invitation to attend a reception following the service is included.

ORDINATION
OF A MINISTER

Service One

Pastor: Here we are, Lord.

Congregation: Yes, here we are, in the name of Jesus Christ. We know that we do not love God as much as we should. We don't really love our brothers and sisters as much as we love ourselves. We are sorry for this, but still, here we are—begging God's forgiveness and looking to God to help us.

Pastor: Dear Lord, heal us. Help us to love more than we do.

Congregation: Holy Spirit, come into our hearts. We want your Presence to fill us to overflowing. We are here, Lord, and we earnestly and sincerely desire this precious gift.

(Silence for a few minutes)

Pastor: Hear the Word of the Lord. *(Reading of Scripture)*

Congregation: Amen.

Pastor: Praise the Lord! Praise the Lord!

Congregation: We do praise the Lord. He is worthy of our praise, and we will love him and praise him for all our lives.

Pastor: God, in his generous mercy, has sent _____ to serve you as your pastor. *He* is a *man,* but *he* comes to you with the blessing of almighty God.

Congregation: We accept _____ as our pastor and we thank God for *him*.

Pastor: Be assured that *he* is a *man* of God who relies heavily on the Savior. *He* needs your love and your prayers.

Congregation: We will love *him* and help *him* and pray with *him* and for *him*.

Pastor: God will uphold *him* in this ministry.

Congregation: And we will love *him*.

Pastor: (To the candidate) _____, you have promised to serve these people as their pastor. Do you accept this responsibility?

Candidate: Yes, I humbly and willingly accept it.

Pastor: (To the congregation) You have promised to support and love _____ as your pastor. Do you accept this responsibility?

Congregation: Yes, we humbly and willingly accept it.

Pastor: Then go, all of you, and serve the Lord with joy in your hearts.

Congregation: We praise the Lord!

Service Two

Note: This adapted service is for the ordination and installation of an assistant pastor in the Lutheran Church, but could be easily changed to fit any Protestant church.

Presentor: I present for ordination to the Holy Ministry _____, who has been properly prepared, examined, and certified by the Church, and who has been called to the office of Assistant Pastor-Worker-Priest in _____ church.

People: We thank God.

Pastor: According to apostolic usage you are now to be set apart for the ministry of the Word and sacraments by the laying on of hands and prayer. Hear then, what our Lord Jesus Christ says: "Peace be with you. As the Father has sent me, even so I send you. . . . Receive the Holy Spirit. If you forgive the sins of any, they are forgiven; if you retain the sins of any, they are retained" [John 20:21 RSV]. And again, "All authority in heaven and on earth has been given to me. Go therefore and make disciples of all nations, baptizing them in the name of the Father and of the Son and of the Holy Spirit, teaching them to observe all that I have commanded you; and lo, I am with you always, to the close of the age." [Matt. 28:18-20 RSV]

Pastor: (To the candidate) Are you persuaded that the Lord has called you to the ministry of Word and sacraments, and are you willing to assume this office?

Response: Yes, I am called by the Lord and I am willing to answer that call.

Pastor: The church in which you are to be ordained confesses that the Holy Scriptures are the written Word of God and the only judge, rule, and norm of faith and life. We believe, teach and confess the Apostles, Nicene, and Athanasian creeds and acknowledge the Lutheran confessions as true witnesses and faithful expositions of the Holy Scriptures. Will you therefore preach and teach in accordance with the Holy Scriptures and these confessions?

Response: I will.

Pastor: Will you be diligent in your use of the means of grace? Will you pray for God's people and

nourish them with his Word and holy sacraments, leading them in faithful service and holy living?
Response: Yes, I will, with the help of God.
Pastor: May the Lord who has given you the will to do these things, graciously give you the strength and compassion to perform them.
Congregation: Amen.
THE LAYING ON OF HANDS: *(Candidate kneels; pastor lays hand on candidate's head)*
Pastor: Eternal God, pour out your Holy Spirit upon _____, your servant, whom you have called to be a pastor. Add power to *his* proclamation of your Word so that the church may be renewed and strengthened. Increase the gifts of your Spirit in *his* life. Give *him* wisdom to equip your people for their work of ministry, for building up the body of Christ. To your name be the glory.
Congregation: Amen.
Pastor: It is announced now that _____ is ordained a minister of the Word and sacraments in the church of Jesus Christ.
Congregation: Amen. Thanks be to God.
Pastor: To *him* is committed the pastoral office with the authority to preach the Word and administer the sacraments; in the name of the Father and of the Son and of the Holy Spirit.
Congregation: Amen.
Pastor: (Removes hand from candidate's head and candidate stands. Pastor hands the candidate a Bible) Receive these Holy Scriptures as a sign and token of your calling to preach and teach the Word of God faithfully.
Pastor: (Hands candidate a stole) Receive this stole as a sign of your working together with Christ Jesus. Walk in obedience to him in your service

among his people, remembering his promise: "Come
to me, all who labor and are heavy laden, and I will
give you rest. Take my yoke upon you, and learn
from me; for I am gentle and lowly in heart, and you
will find rest for your souls. For my yoke is easy, and
my burden is light." [Matt. 11:28 RSV] Care for
God's people; bear their burdens, do not betray their
confidences. So discipline yourself in life and
teaching that you preserve the truth, giving no
occasion for false security or illusory hope. And be of
good courage, for God himself has called you, and
your labor in the Lord will not be in vain.

The Rite of Installation

Pastor: Having been authorized by the Church to
install _____, our co-worker in the gospel, as
Assistant Pastor-Worker-Priest, I now ask for
certification of his call.
Chairman of the Congregation: We, of _____
Church, certify that _____ has been duly called to
be assistant-pastor-worker-priest.
Pastor: (To the candidate) Are you ready to assume
the office of assistant pastor-worker-priest in this
congregation?
Response: Yes, I am.
Pastor: Will you be faithful in your ministry? Will
you be diligent in your use of the means of grace?
Will you preach and teach in accordance with the
Holy Scriptures? Will you pray for God's people and
nourish them with the Word of God and the
sacraments, leading them in faithful service and
holy living?
Response: Yes, I will, with the help of God.

Pastor: The Lord who has given you the will to do these things will graciously give you the strength and compassion to perform them.

Congregation: Amen.

Pastor: And you, the people of God, will you receive _____, a messenger of Jesus Christ, sent by God and ordained to serve his people with the message of hope and salvation? Will you pray for *him,* help and honor *him* for *his* work's sake, and in all things strive to live together in peace and unity in Christ?

Congregation: We will, and we ask God to help us.

Pastor: Upon these solemn promises I now declare _____ to be assistant pastor-worker-priest of_____ church; in the name of the Father, and of the Son, and of the Holy Spirit. Amen.

Congregation: Amen.

INSTALLATION OF A PASTOR

Service One

Officer of the Congregation: We have met together today in worship to consider our common mission and ministry as God's people. We have heard the Scriptures and the Address. The charge and response have been given in our hearing. Now we solemnly enter into this Covenant of Installation. Will the members of this church please stand and responsively repeat our Covenant with our minister.

Minister: I have been called by God to be a minister of the church of Jesus Christ, and I come to you, ready to be your minister in his behalf.

Congregation: We are called by God to be the church of Jesus Christ, and we welcome you and receive you as Christ's minister and ours.

Minister: I covenant with you to be your preacher and teacher, to speak to you the Word of God as it comes to me through the Scriptures and reason, and as it comes to me in my experiences in the community of faith and the community of humanity, and as it comes to me by the inspiration of the Holy Spirit.

Congregation: We covenant with you to be seekers after the Word of God, to be earnest hearers and diligent students, searching always for his will in our lives, believing there is yet more truth to come from his living Word.

Minister: I covenant with you to be your pastor and your friend, your counselor and companion in both the agonies and the ecstasies of life, the sorrows and joys, the defeats and the triumphs, sharing regularly with you in the ministry of prayer.

Congregation: We covenant with you, and with one another, to share with you and to support you in our common ministry and pastoral concern for our members and friends, and all others such as God would lead to us. We will pray regularly for you and for one another.

Minister: I covenant with you to mediate to you the grace and acceptance of God, to speak not only the prophetic word of law and judgment, but to speak even more the word of forgiveness and love. I will, God helping me, encourage you to maintain all faith, love and hope, in your personal lives, and to strive for the love and justice of the kingdom of God in your social life.

Congregation: We covenant with you to strive, God helping us, to be a community of grace, to receive God's word of judgment, as well as his word of mercy and forgiveness. We will support you in our common cause for love and justice in the world, maintaining always a free pulpit, wherein the truth of God, as you understand it, may be spoken unhindered.

Minister: With a heart filled with thanksgiving I accept my call from you as a call from God. I regard it as a great honor and high privilege to enter into this covenant and relationship with you. I humbly present myself to you, in the name of Christ our Lord, for formal installation as your minister for as long as it seems good both to us and to the Holy Spirit.

Congregation: After careful consideration and much prayer, we have called you to leadership. We sincerely believe this is the call of God. For our common mission and ministry we pledge our faithful support with our prayers, abilities, and money. Therefore, in the name of the Father, and the Son, and the Holy Spirit, we do hereby formally install you as our minister for as long as it seems good to us and to the Holy Spirit. May God bless you and us as we serve him together.

Officer of the Congregation: In keeping with ancient tradition we now extend the right hand of fellowship to our pastor, sealing our covenant with *him.*

THE RIGHT HAND OF FELLOWSHIP: *The officer of the congregation and other participants give the minister the right hand of fellowship. The minister will then proceed down the aisles, giving the*

*right hand of fellowship to each person at the end of
each pew, who in turn will pass the handshake down
the row until all in the congregation have partici-
pated in this covenant ceremony.*

Service Two

Officiant: Oh God, our eternal, loving Father, we
ask for the presence of your Holy Spirit here in this
place today as we renew our congregational
covenant with you and as we celebrate a new
covenant between pastor and people. Bless us so
that a spirit of openness and love will prevail as we
dedicate ourselves to service to one another and to
the world you love, through Jesus Christ our Lord.
Congregation: Amen.
(President of the Church Council comes forward)
AFFIRMATION OF PURPOSE OF THE
    CONGREGATION:
President: As a congregation we have been called
for a purpose: to engage as many persons as will
share our confession of faith in a fellowship of
worship, learning, witness, and service, that the
Word of God in Jesus Christ may become effective in
our lives together and individually, including
relationships with other Christian fellowships at
home and throughout the world. Will you, my fellow
members of this church, affirm this purpose?
Congregation: We do so affirm. This is our mission
and our task.
President: Will we continue to nurture our members, young and old, in worship, learning and the
development of our ministries?
Congregation: Yes, with the help of God.

President: Will we continue to work together through faith, active in love for justice and the meeting of human need in the local and wider community?

Congregation: Yes, with the help of God.

President: Will we participate in and support mission through the channels of the wider Christian community, and will we strive to go beyond minimal expectations?

Congregation: Yes, with the help of God.

President: Will we work and pray together as a parish family so that we may provide facilities and resources to further all these functions?

Congregation: Yes, with the help of God.

President: May the Lord of the Church make us mindful of our calling and give us openness to evaluate our faithfulness to this mission.

Congregation: Amen.

(Pastor-elect comes forward)

AFFIRMATION OF CALL BY CONGREGATION:

Officiant: To enable the church in its ministry, God has provided pastors. Upon recommendation of the church council, a *man* has now been called to this church to serve as our pastor. We hear now the expectations of this congregation as given in the formal call.

EPISTLE: *(Right side)* As pastor of this congregation, you will be required to preach and teach the Word of God, to conduct public worship, to administer the sacraments, to maintain Christian discipline, and to be a true shepherd to the members of this congregation; to lead and direct the work of the congregation and to perform the duties of the gospel ministry as becomes one called to that holy office.

GOSPEL: *(Left side)* You will further be expected to try to extend the kingdom of God in this community, in the United States and elsewhere; to impart knowledge of the church and its wider ministry; to endeavor to increase the liberality of the congregation in the support of the work of the church at large. *Congregation:* We pledge to you our prayers, our love and esteem and also the full use of all resources of spirit and means for the furtherance of the kingdom of God so long as you continue to be our pastor, and we assume responsibility for the temporal support and comfort of you and your family.

(Congregation is seated. Members of the church council present themselves at the chancel)

INSTALLATION RITE:

Officiant: In addition to the expectations voiced by the members of this congregation, you will also be responsible as the pastor of this church to carry out the following duties: care for your people individually and as a congregation, give catechetical instructions, confirm, instruct new members, and supervise all the schools of the congregation; marry persons in accordance with the teaching of the church and the laws of the state; visit the sick and the distressed, bury the dead; inculcate piety individually and corporately; install regularly elected members of the church council; administer discipline; seek out and encourage qualified young men and women to prepare for the ministry of the gospel. And now, brothers and sisters in Christ, having been authorized by the church to install _____, our fellow laborer in the gospel, as pastor of this congregation I now ask for certification of *his* call.

President: This is to certify that the Reverend
_____ has been called as pastor of _____ at a
special congregational meeting held on _____.

Officiant: Since you have been called as pastor of
this congregation and now present yourself before
the Lord and his people to be installed in this office,
hear and consider with us the promises and
admonitions of Holy Scripture.

*Evangelism Committee Chairperson: (Read Acts
1:7-8)*

*Social Ministry Committee Chairperson: (Read
John 12:26)*

*Youth Committee Chairperson: (Read II Timothy
4:5)*

*Worship and Music Committee Chairperson: (Read
John 14:27)*

*Property Committee Chairperson: (Read Luke
22:26)*

*Stewardship Committee Chairperson: (Read John
21:15)*

Officiant: The Lord grant you grace to faithfully
keep these words in your heart; may they guide you
in your daily work and conversation and ever
remind you of your responsibility; may they
increase your worthiness and inspire you with zeal
in your continued service for our Chief Shepherd.

The church looks to you always to bear in mind
the important and sacred responsibility of the office
entrusted to you this day and expects you to
continue in earnest prayer to God for grace to fulfill
the same—that you may prove a good and faithful
servant of the Lord.

I ask you now, do you accept the office and
ministry to which you have been called by this
congregation?

Pastor: I do.

Officiant: Will you try to serve faithfully, always to the glory of God and to the well-being of his holy Church?

Pastor: Yes, I will, with the help of God.

(Congregation stands)

Officiant: Brothers and sisters in Christ, you have heard the pledge of this person whom you have called to be your pastor. I ask you: will you receive *him,* and give *him* love and support as one who serves with you as a shepherd and teacher? Will you honor *him* as Paul has exhorted—know those who labor with you, sent by the Lord to lead you, and support them for the sake of the gospel?

Congregation: Yes, with the help of God.

Officiant: May almighty God strengthen and help you to keep these promises.

(The pastor-elect kneels)

Officiant: The office of pastor of _____ church is now committed to you; in the name of the Father, Son, and Holy Spirit. The Lord be with you.

Pastor-Elect and Congregation: And with your spirit.

Officiant: Almighty God, you have ordained that men and women might serve in special ways to fulfill a ministry for the church of your dear Son. We thank you that you have given to this congregation _____, as pastor and teacher. We ask that you enrich *him* with your grace, that faithfully fulfilling *his* ministry *his* labors may be blessed, to the enlightening of men, women, and children.

Congregation: Amen. (The Lord's Prayer)

Officiant: The Lord bless you in your ministry so that Jesus Christ will be honored here.

Congregation: Amen.

Service Three

Pastor: It is good to see all of you here, but why are you here?

People: We are here to praise God for all of the wondrous things he has done for us.

Pastor: After you praise him, what will you do?

People: We will seek to learn of his will in our lives.

Pastor: After you learn of his will, what will you do?

People: We will go forth to serve God and his church.

(Prayer—spoken together)

O Lord, you never fail to help and to guide those who open their lives to you. Help us to see always what the real needs of our lives are, and reveal yourself as sufficient to meet those needs. We pray in the name of your Son, our Lord. Amen.

THE READING OF THE WORD OF GOD: *(Read I Thessalonians 5:12-13)*

RESPONSIVE READING: *(Read Psalm 67)*

THE READING OF THE WORD OF GOD: *(Read Romans 12:1-8)*

THE INSTALLATION:

Pastor: Dear friends in Christ, I ask you if you accept _____ as your shepherd and leader to minister to you.

Congregation: Yes, we have called *him* to be our pastor.

Pastor: Will you pray for and with *him,* support *his* ministry, help *him* when asked, and most of all, will you love *him*?

Congregation: Oh yes, we promise to do all these things.

Pastor: (To candidate) You have heard the promises of these people. Will you enter into this ministry wholeheartedly, serving the Lord with all your strength?

Candidate: Yes, I promise.

Pastor: Will you stand ready at all times to serve these people, whether in prayer, with consolation, in celebration, to meet their needs, in the name of Jesus Christ?

Candidate: Yes, I want to serve them.

Pastor: Then I declare you to be installed as the pastor of this congregation. Be at peace and go with God.

Congregation: Amen.

INSTALLATION OF A REGIONAL MINISTER (OR A DISTRICT PRESIDENT, OR A BISHOP)

THE CHURCH IN THE DISTRICT:

Leader: I invite the [district moderators, representatives of departments and committees] to rise and make their covenant.

Response: As members of the [district] we affirm our significant role in the life and work of the regional church. We covenant together to support the regional program of ministry to congregations by being sensitive links between the local congregation and the regional staff. We offer to our [regional minister] our prayers and our energy in the task of building the Body of Christ in the region and we look forward to his counsel and his ministry with us.

Leader: Thank you for that expression of support.

THE CHURCH IN THE REGION:

Leader: I invite the members of the [regional board and executive committee] to rise and make their covenant.

Response: As members of the administrative board of the region, we covenant with our [regional minister] to be willing participants in the task of leading the Christian Church in this state. We pledge to listen to *him,* learn from *him,* and offer *him* our wisest counsel. We will support *him* with our prayers, encouragement, friendship, and love. In all things we give to *him* the gift of assistance in developing the region as the Church Triumphant.

Leader: Thank you for that expression of support.

THE CLERGY:

Leader: I invite the clergy of the _____ Church in this state to rise and make their covenant.

Response: As pastors and teachers of the faith in our congregations we covenant with our regional minister to share with *him* in the task of enabling the church to minister to the world, through the proclamation, teaching, and healing of the gospel, and through the celebration of God's participation in the daily events of human life. We look to *him* as counselor and leader, *brother* and helper. Earnestly, we covenant to work together as clergy to the end that the congregations we serve shall share responsibility in the task of the whole Body of Christ, the increase of love of God and neighbor in the world.

Leader: Thank you for that expression of support.

THE CONGREGATIONS:

Leader: I invite the members of the congregations of the _____ Church in this state to rise and make their covenant.

Response: Affirming our membership in the Church of Jesus Christ and our fellowship in the family of the Church, the congregations which are the _____ Church in this state, we renew our confession of faith in our Lord Jesus Christ, and his Church. Believing in the priesthood of all believers, we covenant with our [regional minister] to work alongside *him* in the faith and nurture of all our congregations, to seek *his* counsel in the call of a pastor, to support *his* leadership in strengthening the witness of our congregations, to increase the love of God and neighbor in the world.

Leader: Thank you for that expression of support.

REGIONS AND INSTITUTIONS:

Leader: I invite the representatives from the regions and institutions of the _____ Church to rise and make their covenant.

Response: We affirm the oneness of the church and its common ministry through the various general units of the church. We join hands in this ministry with the [regional minister] and covenant our support of him as a colleague and friend in extending the ministry of Christ in mission, witness and service among the people and social structures of this state, country and the world.

Leader: Thank you for that expression of support.

OUR GENERAL MINISTER AND PRESIDENT:

(A short address by the president, in person or on tape)

THE CHURCH ECUMENICAL:

Leader: I invite ecumenical guests to rise and make their covenant.

Response: We bring greetings on this occasion from our judicatories in this state. Affirming the oneness of the Church ecumenically, we welcome the [regional minister] of the _____ Church, and as a co-worker in ministry to and with the whole body of Christ. We covenant to be open to *his* leadership and to opportunities to witness together to the good news of Jesus Christ as the Church Universal.

Leader: Thank you for that statement of greeting and support.

THE RESPONSE BY THE REGIONAL MINISTER.

Leader: May the mighty God, our Lord, bless and keep you forever. May you know peace, perfect peace, and courage in everything you try to do for him. Lift up your hearts, look up and see his dear face and know his grace. He will bless you forever. Amen.

ORDINATION AND INSTALLATION OF ELDERS AND DEACONS

Minister: There are different gifts in the ministry of Christ's Church, different skills and interests, different temperaments and personalities.

People: But we serve the same Lord. God works through each of us according to our capabilities.

Minister: We are given different gifts by the Spirit of God for the upbuilding of the Church and the saving restoration of humanity.

People: Some of us carry on the Christian tradition by teaching; others by listening and responding; some by social action, others by serving in the community; some by maintaining a church building, others by creating small groups; some by the strength of their worship and prayer, others by the making of fellowship. Though we have different gifts, we serve the same Lord.

Minister: Within our common ministry, some members are chosen for particular work as elders and deacons. Elders are elected to support the ministry of the church in its government and in its program. Deacons are elected to maintain the church as an institution and to provide for its stewardship. Elders and deacons are to be worship leaders. They take final responsibility for the quality of the witness of this church to the God of Jesus Christ in this community.

(President introduces the elders and deacons)

Minister: God has called you through the Church to serve Jesus Christ in a special way. Do you trust in the God of Jesus Christ as head of the Church, and do you accept the meaning and power of the biblical witness in your lives, and do you believe the Christian Church has a mission relevant to the chaos and the opportunities of this time?

Candidates: Yes, I do.

Minister: Will you exercise your ministry as human and fragile, but committed, students of the Christian faith, keeping the priorities of Church and world in perspective, ministering to people and groups, opening the congregation to all who would enter, and continually seeking deeper and more meaningful ways of doing the Lord's work?

Candidates: Yes, I will.

Minister: Will you seek to serve the people with energy, intelligence, imagination, love, tolerance, and good humor?

Candidates: Yes, I will.

President: (Of the congregation) Do we, members of the church, accept these new officers chosen by God through the voice of this congregation, to lead us in the work of the God of Jesus Christ?

People: Yes, we do.

President: Do we promise to support them by continual concern, helpful words and acts, and volunteer time, and do we put our trust in them to represent us?

People: Yes, we do.

(Candidates kneel)

Minister: Take authority to execute the office of Elder and Deacon in the Church of Jesus Christ to which I now entrust you.

Almighty God, in every time you have chosen servants to speak your word and lead your people. We thank you for these people whom you have called to serve you. Grant them gifts to do their work. Make these leaders wise and faithful, humble and prophetic, patient and persevering, self-critical and full of humor, glad to be what they are and expecting much from their life in the Church.

Candidates: God, our Father, you have chosen us. Now give us strength, wisdom, and love to fulfill our calling.

People: God of grace, give us courage and discipline to follow and to lead, that as one congregation we may make your acts known in this place and in the world.

Minister: You are now Elders and Deacons in this church and the leadership of this congregation. Whatever you do, in word or act, do everything in the name of the Lord, giving thanks to God. Claim your ministry. Rejoice in the work you have been given. Look to the future with hope.

People: Amen.

INSTALLATION OF OFFICERS
OF THE CHURCH

Charge: You have been elected by the fellow members of this church to serve as officers and leaders, and you have declared your willingness to serve. Do you accept the responsibilities of the office into which you are installed and do you promise to faithfully and efficiently discharge your duties?
Response: I do, God enabling me.
Charge: Will you seek to promote and maintain a sympathetic and friendly relationship with those with whom you work, so that the bond of fellowship throughout the church may be strengthened?
Response: I do, God enabling me.
Charge: Do you promise to be faithful to your church, consistent in your attendance, dutiful in your support of the total church program?
Response: I do, God enabling me.
Charge: Do you promise to honor God and your church in your service, behavior and conduct?
Response: I do, God enabling me.
Charge to the Congregation: The responsibilities which these officers and leaders are now called upon to assume cannot be discharged by them alone. They have promised to serve their offices well, God enabling them, but their best efforts will fail unless they are supported by the whole-hearted and consistent cooperation of the entire congregation.

Do you, members of this congregation, acknowledge and receive these officers and leaders as duly elected officers? Do you promise to give them the honor, encouragement, and cooperation to which their offices entitle them? If so, signify by standing.

To the Officers: I now declare you duly inducted into the offices to which you have been elected. May the grace of God be with you, and may you enjoy the confidence and loving support of your fellow members.

RECEPTION OF NEW MEMBERS

Pastor: (To the new members) You have applied for membership in this congregation: you have met with the pastor(s), who has conveyed your sincerity to the church council, and your request for membership has been heartily approved. I want you to know that you are joining a worshiping, learning, witnessing, and serving community of baptized persons among whom the Word is proclaimed and the sacraments are celebrated according to the gospel. As members here, your Christian lifestyle will be aided by what you receive through worship and your contributions to the ongoing ministry of the church. Your faith will be nurtured by participation in continuing adult education and through discussions with your brothers and sisters in the faith. You will witness to your faith in your work and play, among your family, friends, and enemies; and in bearing the name of Jesus Christ.

And, in taking the name of Christ, you have agreed to serve and be served. Some opportunities for this service will be offered here. Others you will discover and do on your own. All of them, known and unknown, are a part of God's glue that holds us together.

In addition to your worshiping, learning, witnessing, and serving, you are encouraged to frequently celebrate Holy Communion, your opportunity to be fed and forgiven as sons and daughters of God. And, as you were baptized and belong to the Great Tradition, your children, too, will be included in that continuing story.

You will be challenged to underwrite with your money a worldwide ministry that reaches far beyond this country's borders and deeply into local community programs.

I ask you now, will you, through this congregation, minister and be ministered to, spill your cup for others and allow it to be filled, care about others and permit them to care for you, and all this, in the faith of your baptism? If so, answer "Yes, by the help of God."

(Congregation rises)

Pastor: I now ask you, members of this congregation, will you welcome these persons into our fellowship, aiding, helping, befriending, and caring about them as they share their gifts of mind, muscle and money with your own? If you do, answer "Yes, with the help of God."

Gladly we welcome you into membership of this church, and we ask you to join us as together we confess the faith into which we have been baptized.

All: (Recite the Apostles' Creed)

CELEBRATING
THE INSTALLATION OF THE BOARD
OF GOVERNING OFFICERS

Pastor: Lord, we are here together in your house today to install the officers of our congregation. We pray for your blessing on them and the work they will attempt during this coming year.

_____, _____, _____, and _____, I speak to you. As I think about your office and the work this congregation has entrusted to you, I am reminded of the verse in Scripture that speaks of Christ, "Who shall change our vile body, that it may be fashioned like unto his glorious body, according to the working whereby he is able even to subdue all things unto himself." [Phil. 3:21 KJV]

A caterpillar is a rather vile creature. It lives in the dirt and mud and slithers along on its belly. It is like a sinner before he accepts the Lord Jesus Christ as his Savior. Before a sinner can accept Jesus, he has to know that he is in a very low, vile position, like the caterpillar. His eyes are always looking down.

However, the caterpillar goes through some wonderful and marvelous changes, and a lovely butterfly emerges. And we too must be transformed, changed, by Christ. The butterfly is always looking up.

What kind of leaders will you be? How will you approach the problems that will surely arise in this congregation during the coming year?

Will you have a wormy, down-in-the-mouth attitude, saying that nothing will turn out anyway, so why try? Will you slither away from responsibilities with hastily made up excuses? Will you burrow into your hole when difficulties arise?

Or will you be like the butterfly, poised at the beginning of this year with fluttering wings, your eyes looking up toward a Savior who will bless and sustain you? Like a butterfly who soars upward, happy to be alive, grateful to be free?

We want butterflies, not caterpillars. We have elected you to serve this congregation as officers who will solve problems for us, make important decisions for us, tell us when things are not going well, and encourage us when things look bleak. We want you to have the courage of your own convictions and to impart some of that courage and hopefulness to us. We pray that you will approach your tasks in this way, and we have every confidence that you will.

Congregation: Amen.

Pastor: (To officers) Do you promise to do your very best, relying heavily on the Lord for support, to run the affairs of this congregation?

Officers: With the help of God, we will do our best.

Pastor: Dear people of this congregation, will you help and encourage these officers in their work and will you pray for their success?

Congregation: Yes, we will do that.

Pastor: Then I declare that _____, _____, _____, and _____ are the official members of the Governing Board of this church and I ask God's blessing for them and for us.

Congregation: Amen.

Pastor: Go with peace and joy in your hearts.

INSTALLATION
OF PARISH LEADERS

Pastor: (To the members of the vestry) By the power of God's Holy Spirit, he has raised up his Holy Church to be the people of the new covenant, and the living sign of his presence among us. The Church is the family of God, the Body of Christ, and the temple of the Holy Spirit. All baptized people are called to make Christ known as Savior and Lord, and to share in the renewing of his world.

As vestry/lay ministers/elders, it is our mutual privilege to proclaim by word and deed the gospel of Jesus Christ, and to fashion our lives in accordance with its precepts. We are to love and serve the people of this parish, caring alike for young and old, strong and weak, rich and poor. We are to be the chief channels through which God's love and wisdom, his forgiveness and his strength, are to be known in this place.

As the leaders of this congregation, we are to nourish Christ's people from the riches of his grace, and to strengthen them to glorify God in this life and in the life to come. Do you now, in the presence of God's holy people, dedicate yourself to this trust and responsibility?

Vestry: I do.

Pastor: Will you respect, and be guided by, the pastoral direction and leadership of the church and be loyal to its doctrines, disciplines, and worship?

Vestry: Yes, I will.

Pastor: Will you be diligent in the reading and study of the Holy Scriptures, and in seeking the knowledge of such things as may make you stronger and more able ministers of Christ?

Vestry: Yes, I will.

Pastor: Will you undertake to be faithful ministers to all whom you are called to serve, laboring together with them and your fellow ministers to build up the family of God?

Vestry: Yes, I will.

Pastor: Will you do your best to pattern your lives, and those of your families and households, in accordance with the teachings of Christ, so that you may be a wholesome example to this congregation?

Vestry: Yes, I will.

Pastor: Will you persevere in prayer, in public and in private, asking God's grace, both for yourselves and for others, offering all your labors to God, through the mediation of Jesus Christ, and in the sanctification of the Holy Spirit?

Vestry: Yes, I will.

(The congregation stands and the pastor addresses them)

Pastor: My brothers and sisters in Christ, out of your charity, pray for the vestry of this church. Pray that the Lord our God will bless them with the fullness of his love making them faithful ministers of Christ; that they may serve his church and the world for which he died, in holiness and faithfulness.

People: Lord, hear our prayer.

Pastor: In your kindness, pray also for me, that despite my unworthiness, I may faithfully fulfill the office of priest and pastor which Jesus Christ has entrusted to me. Pray that I may become more and more like Christ, our great high priest, the shepherd and bishop of our souls, the teacher and servant of all; and that I may minister to the unity and peace of God's one holy and apostolic Church.

People: Lord, listen to our prayer.

Pastor: And pray for yourselves and for all the holy people of God, here and throughout the world, that we may show forth the power of Christ in all that we do, offering to God our heavenly Father the pleasing sacrifice of lives made courageous, just, and holy in the likeness of Jesus Christ our Lord; until, at last, we are brought with all the bright company of the saints to the banquet of eternal glory.

People: Lord, hear our prayer.

Pastor: May God give you power through the Spirit for your hidden self to grow strong, so that Christ may live in your hearts through faith, and so that, planted in love and built on love, you will with all the saints have the strength to grasp the breadth and length, the height and depth; until, knowing the love of Christ, which is beyond all knowledge, you are filled with the utter and complete fullness of God.

All: Glory to him whose power, working in us, can do infinitely more than we can ask or imagine: Glory be to him from generation to generation in the Church and in Christ Jesus for ever and ever. Amen.

CELEBRATING THE INSTALLATION OF A PARISH WORKER

Pastor: We are here today to install _____ as the Parish Worker of our congregation.
Congregation: And we are here to praise the Lord.
Pastor: We are here to celebrate the fact of parish work in our congregation.
Congregation: And we are here to praise God.
Pastor: We are here for several reasons, but mostly to worship and praise God.
Congregation: Amen.
Pastor: As I prepared for this service today I kept thinking about Noah. About how he worked and worked, building that ark, and how people laughed at him and called him crazy. Why did he keep on working and working under clear, dry skies with people laughing at him? Why? Because he believed with all his heart and soul that God would do what he had said he would do. That's all. He believed in what he was doing, so he worked on, ignoring everyone else.

Now I know that none of you will be laughing at _____, or calling *him* crazy, but as *he* goes about *his* work as our parish worker, *he* is going to have some innovative ideas; *he* may try to do the "undo-able" once in a while. *He* will almost certainly call on some of you to do things you never thought of before; because that's *his* job and *he* believes in it, and *he* feels that the Lord wants *him* to accomplish great things in this church.

I know you won't laugh at *him,* but will you turn the other way when *he* asks for your help? Or will you mumble, "It will never work!" when *he* wants to try something a little bit new and different? Will you say to others, "*He*'s crazy to try that"? Will you put thumbs down on anything *he* suggests just because it hasn't been done before?

If you do these things, you won't stop _____. *He* will just keep working because *he* believes in what *he*'s doing and, like Noah, *he* knows what the Lord has told *him* to do. However, you will miss out on something pretty special. Working with *him* will open your eyes to a lot of possibilities and great things just might happen in this parish. So, dear people of this congregation, are you willing to be open to _____'s ideas and opportunities and to assist *him* in every possible way?

Congregation: Yes, we are.

Pastor: _____, since the congregation has expressed its desire and intention to support you in your work as Parish Worker of this congregation, are you willing to accept the responsibility, and will you promise to work under the Lord's direction and for the good of this congregation?

Candidate: Yes, I am willing and I so promise.

Pastor: Then, in the eyes of God, and with your promises and the promises of this congregation in mind, I see nothing but good in this relationship; and I pronounce you the Parish Worker of this congregation.

Congregation: Amen.

Pastor: Leave this place now with joy in your hearts, courage to try new things for Christ, and confidence that he will bless you in a mighty way.

RITE OF INSTALLATION FOR A DIRECTOR OF CHRISTIAN EDUCATION

Pastor: Our Lord Jesus instituted the office of the holy ministry in his Church on earth. He appointed some to be apostles, others to be prophets, others to be evangelists, others to be pastors and teachers to prepare God's people for the work of Christian service, to build up the Body of Christ.

To qualify and equip us for such offices, God gives special gifts. The ability to perform these functions comes from God alone, as Paul writes: "we have confidence in God through Christ. There is nothing in us that allows us to claim that we are capable of doing this work. The capacity we have comes from God; it is he who made us capable of serving the new covenant." [II Cor. 3:4-6 TEV]

Our Lord has not promised to give this ability directly, but he gives it through his Holy Spirit by means of the instruction and training of his sacred Word.

Our Lord taught his disciples for three years and then gave them the commission to teach everything he had commanded them. Paul faithfully instructed Timothy and other servants of the Word and charged them, as he wrote to Timothy: "What you have heard from me before many witnesses entrust to faithful men who will be able to teach others also." [II Tim. 2:2 RSV] As our Lord instructed his Church and its ministers to teach his Word to all, young and old, to nurture and tend both his lambs and his sheep, our congregation conducts and maintains programs of Christian Education and Youth Ministry for its members. In order to improve and expand this work of Christian Education and Youth Ministry, the congregation has, in a regular meeting, called upon God for guidance, and acting in his fear, resolved to call a Director of Christian Education and Youth Ministry.

Our call has been extended to you, _____, and you have accepted it. As our Director of Christian Education and Youth Ministry you, together with the Board of Christian Education of this congregation, are to plan, promote and train teachers and leaders, supervise and evaluate all agencies and endeavors of Christian Education in such a way that the teaching and learning of God's Word in this congregation constantly improves and expands to reach more and more people.

In this work you are to be associated with the pastor and the elders, who are concerned for and charged with the total Christian ministry. To this office you have been called by God to apply yourself with all diligence and consecration, in public and in private. The Lord of the Church would also, by your faithful service and ministry, build his Church. In this charge and task it will therefore be your comfort that your office is of God, and the Lord Jesus Christ himself will be with you, as he has promised his faithful servants.

By divine guidance you have recognized in this call the voice of God and are about to enter into the duties of your important office, for whose faithful performance you will be held accountable to God, and I ask you in the presence of God and this congregation: Are you ready, after mature and prayerful consideration, to assume the office of Director of Christian Education and Youth Ministry in this congregation and to fulfill its duties according to the ability God gives?

Candidate: I am ready.

Pastor: Do you promise to order your life and your teaching, and also the performance of all the duties of your office, faithfully according to the Word of God and the confessions of our church?

Candidate: I promise, and I pray for God's help.

Pastor: In testimony of your sincerity in making this promise, give me your right hand.

Pastor: (To the congregation) Dear brothers and sisters, you have heard the solemn promise given by _____, whom you have called to be your Director of Christian Education and Youth Ministry. I admonish and charge you to receive *him* in this office and to be mindful of what God's Word says to you.

Attend with all diligence the instruction in God's Word offered you in this congregation, and receive it not as the word of human beings, but, as it is in truth, the Word of God. Heed his admonition and accept with meekness the divine Word he plants in your hearts, which is able to save your souls.

Help *him* and cooperate with *him* in all Christian Education endeavors, also in the instruction of the young; and remember that as Christians you are to bring up your children in the discipline and instruction of the Lord. Honor and love *him,* as Paul says, "Respect those who labor among you and are over you in the Lord and admonish you, and . . . esteem them very highly in love because of their work." [I Thess. 5:12 RSV]

Pray for *him* without ceasing that in *his* labors

and concerns *he* may keep a cheerful spirit and *his* ministry among you may be abundantly blessed.

Provide for *his* temporal needs, for the Lord says, "A worker should be given his pay." [Luke 10:7 TEV] And Paul writes: "Let him who is taught the word share all good things with him who teaches." [Gal. 6:6 RSV]

Finally, remember the words of the Apostle: "Obey your leaders and submit to them, for they are keeping watch over your souls, as men who will have to give account. Let them do this joyfully, and not sadly, for that would be of no advantage to you." [Heb. 13:17 RSV]

I now ask you, members of this congregation, are you willing to receive _____ as your Director of Christian Education and Youth Ministry and as a servant of God, and will you show *him* such love, honor, and fit obedience in the Lord as are due an overseer and guide given you by the Lord Jesus Christ, the chief shepherd of souls?

Congregation: We are willing.

(The person to be installed shall kneel and the installing pastor, laying a hand on the candidate's head, shall say)

Pastor: Dear friend, in accordance with your call, I now install you as the Director of Christian Education and Youth Ministry of this congregation, in the name of the Father and the Son and the Holy Spirit. I charge you to be diligent and faithful in the performance of your duties, as you shall give account of your stewardship in the day of Christ's appearing.

Now may the God of peace equip you with everything good that you may do his will.

(The assisting clergy, in turn, may lay their right

hands on the head of the newly installed director and pronounce a similar benediction. Then the newly installed director shall rise, and the installing clergy, giving the director a right hand, shall say)
Pastor: Go then, dear friend, and faithfully perform your work among the sheep and lambs of Christ. Assist us, the pastors, in feeding the whole flock with the Word of God and with sound teaching. Encourage young and old to support and participate in Christian education. Assist parents in bringing up their children in the discipline and instruction of the Lord. Train and equip all our teachers and leaders for their tasks. Take charge of your responsibilities and tasks willingly, as God wants you to. Do your work, not for mere pay, but from a real desire to serve. Do not try to rule over those who have been given into your care, but be a good example. The Lord bless you and make you a blessing to many, so that you may bring forth much fruit and your fruit may remain until the end of time.

To the end that our gracious God may crown the labors of _____ with his blessing, we pray:

Almighty God, you have assigned to your Church the work of Christian Education for your people so that we may be instructed in your word. Continue to use your blessings for all members of this congregation so that your name will be glorified. Give your Holy spirit to _____, and adorn *him* with wisdom and power so that *he* may faithfully perform all the duties of *his* calling. Keep *him* humble, and keep *him* from succumbing to difficulties and discouragements. Help all of us to gladly seek instruction in your Word, and stir up the hearts of the people so that they may cooperate with *him* and with each other. Help *him* and *his* family to be an example of Christian piety and love. Remind us all to pray regularly for each other and for our efforts. Hear us for the sake of your dear Son, Jesus Christ. Amen.

RITE OF INSTALLATION OF SUPERINTENDENT AND BIBLE STUDY LEADER

Pastor: I thank God that you are here. Why did you come?

People: We are here to praise and glorify the Lord.

Pastor: What are you looking for?

People: We are looking for God's blessing on our lives.

Pastor: What else are you looking for?

People: We are asking for a special blessing for _____ and _____, who are being installed as leaders in our church.

Pastor: Let us pray together now and ask God for these blessings.

(Moment of silent prayer)

THE INSTALLATION

Pastor: Will _____ please come forward. As the superintendent of the Christian Education Department of this church you will have many responsibilities. The congregation has elected you to provide a complete Christian Education program so that we may all learn and grow in our faith. Do you understand and accept this responsibility?

Response: Yes, I understand it and I accept it.

Pastor: I exhort you to nurture your own faith so that you will be strong and capable of carrying on this office with which our Lord is well pleased. Will you strive toward this goal?

Response: Yes, I will, and I pray for God's guidance and help.

Pastor: Will _____ please step forward. As the Bible Study leader of this congregation you have an awesome responsibility. This congregation has elected you to bring them a regular schedule of study of the Holy Scriptures for all ages. Do you understand and accept this responsibility?

Response: Yes, I understand it and I accept it.

Pastor: I exhort you to study faithfully the Word of God, whereby he will speak to you so that you will be able to help satisfy the hunger that is in the people of this congregation for the word of God. Will you promise to do this?

Response: Yes, I promise, and I pray that God will make known his wishes to me.

Pastor: And now I speak to you, the members of this congregation. You have thoughtfully and prayerfully considered the candidates for these positions, and you have called _____ and _____ to do the job. Your task is not finished, however. I exhort all of you to support these leaders, to say yes when they ask for your help, to remember them always in your prayers. Will you do these things?

Congregation: Yes, we will, with the help of God.

Pastor: _____ and _____, we welcome you in the service of Jesus Christ in this congregation. We pray that God will bless your work.

Congregation: Amen.

INSTALLATION
OF CHURCH SCHOOL TEACHERS

Minister: Dear Lord, we covet your presence here today as we install the teachers of our church school. Theirs is an awesome responsibility, Lord, bringing your message to the hearts of our dear children, and we pray for your blessings. Give us the love and wisdom to help them when we are asked and impart to them the devotion and love that is needful for this holy task.

Dear members of this congregation, friends, and most especially, teachers; I welcome you on this important day. Why is it so important? After all, we're not installing a president of the church, or even an official board, just a small group of church school teachers. However, in Luke we read that our trust and faith in Jesus Christ will hold us firm. *(Read Luke 6:47-48)*

A firm life. What does that mean? It means a life built on a firm foundation that won't crumble and let us fall at the first sign of trouble. It means being able to live victoriously, fighting the storms of life and remaining our own person in Jesus Christ.

For our children it means that, even though they will see violence, hatred, drugs, adultery, and sin, they will hate these things, and they will have the strength to resist them because their lives are built and nurtured on the solid foundation of faith in Jesus Christ.

As Christians, we will teach our children about the Lord, and we will pray with and for them, and we will try to be the best examples we can; but we know the importance of those Sunday morning hours in church school, too. And we know how blessed we are to have dedicated teachers who are willing to give of themselves to teach our children. Teachers, *(these could be called individually, by name)* do you promise to study the Word of God and to try in every way to bring the truths of the Bible to the children of this congregation?

Response: We will try, and we promise to ask daily for the Lord's help.

Minister: Dear congregation, will you support these teachers in every way that will be required of you?

Response: Yes, we will.

Minister: We welcome these fellow members as teachers of our church school. We ask God to bless their efforts.

Response: Amen.

INSTALLATION OF THE VACATION CHURCH SCHOOL STAFF

The pastor may read the names of those who are to be installed. When the workers have come forward, the vacation school director, or the director of Christian Education, will ask the teachers and leaders to face the audience and will present them to the congregation with these words:

May we present these people who have become partners with you, the members of _____ Church, in the educational ministry of our congregation. They have accepted a call to serve as leaders, teachers, and assistants in our vacation church school.

(Workers turn and face altar)

Pastor: We all have a common concern to increase in our knowledge of Jesus Christ, and to grow in our Christian faith and in our understanding of how God has made us and keeps us in his grace. He has also redeemed us through the life, death, and resurrection of his Son, and promises his Spirit to keep us in the faith. We praise and glorify God for his gifts of love and care.

I ask you to:

—guide and encourage your students to trust their Lord and Savior, Jesus Christ,

—love and accept them as gifts of God for our congregation and community;

—help them to know that all good gifts come from God, and

—help them to responsibly use and share the gifts God gives us.

If these words express your desires and hopes, please say, "Yes, with the help of God."

To you, the members of _____ Church: these people have accepted the call to be your teachers and teach in this congregation and community for you. Will you support their ministry by your prayers, thanks, and encouragement? If so, then answer, "Please accept our thanks. May God bless you."

(Workers at the altar kneel for prayer)

Pastor: Lord God, our Creator in heaven, we thank you that you have revealed yourself to us in your

Son. We are happy that these men and women have responded to your call to serve those who will be attending our vacation church school this year. Add your blessing on what they will plan and do, so that young and old, children and parents, and the whole congregation may grow in Christian faith as they learn to sing your praises and worship together with hearts full of joy. We pray in the name of Jesus. Amen.

Now to him who by the power at work within us is able to do so much more than we can ask or even think, we give all the praise and glory.
Congregation: Amen and amen.

INSTALLATION OF OFFICERS OF A WOMEN'S ORGANIZATION

Service One

Pastor: Women of God, you who are elected and you who consent to be led, I remind you that this women's organization is not an isolated part of the Body of Christ. Listen to some viewpoints on the ministry of women—on your ministry:
A Child's Viewpoint: (The following can be read by children, or by the pastor) The children of this church look to you, the women, to be examples of the life that Jesus taught about and lived. Whenever we see you and hear you, we watch and listen to find Jesus in you.

A Layman's Viewpoint: The men of this church find joy and strength in the faith and ministry of the women of this church. Your leadership in the ministry of women is a blessing not only to the women, but to the men as well.

A Laywoman's Viewpoint: I remind you that we are called to be a community of women who pledge ourselves to know God and to experience freedom as whole persons through Jesus Christ; that we are called to be a fellowship that is creative, and supportive of each woman; that we are called to expand our ideas about ministry and mission by becoming involved in the global ministries of our church.

A Pastor's Viewpoint: As your pastor, I remind you of the liberating ministry of Jesus toward women. As your pastor, I rejoice when I see your acceptance of the ministry to which Jesus Christ calls all Christians. As your pastor, I celebrate the life you give to this church.

The Women's Response: O Lord, we are no longer our own, but yours. Put us to what you will, rank us with whom you will; put us to work, put us to suffering; let us be employed for you or laid aside for you; exalted for you or brought low for you; let us be full, let us be empty! Let us have all things, let us have nothing; we freely and heartily yield all things to your pleasure and disposal.

Pastor: (The elected officers stand) Dearly beloved, you have been called by God, and chosen by these women, to assume special responsibilities in this organization. Your duties include many tasks needful for its welfare and for the advancement of the kingdom of God. Above all, it is your duty, as much as in you lies, to live before all people as becomes the gospel. Having well considered the nature and purpose of the office to which you have been called, will each of you accept this responsibility, and will you seek to accomplish the work and service it sets before you, to the honor and glory of our Lord Jesus Christ?

The Officers' Response: I will, the Lord being my helper.

Pastor: "Therefore my sisters, I implore you by God's mercy to offer your very selves to him: a living sacrifice, dedicated and fit for his acceptance. . . . Adapt yourselves no longer to the pattern of this present world, but let your minds be remade and your whole nature thus transformed. Then you will be able to discern the will of God, and to know what is good, acceptable, and perfect." [Rom. 12:1-2 NEB]

All: Amen.

Pastor: My beloved brothers and sisters, return to your homes with joy in your hearts. Our sisters in the faith have promised to work among us, to the glory of God, and we are assured of Christ's sustaining love and power among us. Go in peace and in joy.

Service Two

The pastor calls the names of all who are to be installed. As each name is called, the person comes forward and faces the congregation.

The pastor then explains the duties of each office. When all have been introduced, and the duties explained, the officers turn and face the pastor.

Pastor: God has called you to be his children. Will you respond to his call?

Officers: Yes, we respond to that call. We look to God as our heavenly Father. We acknowledge him as creator and sustainer of the universe, and we know that he is the source of all life and goodness.

Pastor: Jesus has called you to be his disciples. Will you respond to that call?

Officers: Yes, we respond to that call. We know that Jesus is the Christ, the Savior of us all, and we renew our pledge to follow him.

Pastor: The church has called you to be members of the Body of Christ. Will you respond to its call?

Officers: Yes, we respond to that call. We will remain loyal to the church, and will uphold it with our prayers, our presence, our gifts, and our service.

Pastor: Your fellow members of the *[name of organization]* have called you to be their leaders. Will you respond to their call?

Officers: Yes, we respond to their call. We will do our best to fulfill the duties of the offices to which we have been elected and we will trust in the Lord Jesus Christ for strength.

Pastor: I now declare that you are the officers of the *[name of organization]* in this church. May God bless you and direct you.

Service Three

Note: This is a rather unusual installation service, but one that may be adapted. Do a little research, some searching in the files, to discover the origin of the women's organization in your congregation. This is for a newly organized group, but with some adaptation, the history of the Women's Group—or perhaps any group—could be effectively presented.

Pastor: Once upon a time in the city of _____, there was a church known as _____. And in this congregation there were many women. There were short, tall, fat, and thin ones. There were in-between ones and even perplexed ones. Actually, it was not too colorful a congregation, particularly during the winter. Everyone looked so pale. These women did all sorts of things—washing dishes and the laundry, driving cars, shopping, raising children, and pampering husbands. Others held jobs, some did volunteer work; but the one thing they all had in common was the church.

One day they decided that they needed to be more organized. They wanted to be an active group in their church, to accomplish something for the Lord.

Their first order of the day was to find a leader; not *the* leader, but a chairperson who would see to it that all the bases were covered. The group talked it over and decided what they needed was a chairperson for the committee on nominations. They all pointed to _____ and said, "You're the one for this job, and we'll give you _____ and _____ to help you out."

To have an organization they were certainly going to need members. "How do we go about that?" one of the women asked. And _____ said that she would be at home and close to the phone, and that she would be happy to do what she could about getting others interested in forming a community of women in the church.

The next thought was that these members had to be offered something. "How about resources?" asked _____. "You know, studies, books, a constitution and bylaws and a handbook. We'll need someone to order them and to inform the membership about them." So _____ was asked to be the secretary of program resources, and she was happy to do it. "Since we are all church women, we certainly should devote some of our efforts to mission." Then they appointed mission coordinators to fulfill their purpose. Four were selected: _____, _____, _____, and _____.

The remarkable thing was that everyone they asked to do a job immediately said yes. Surely, the Lord was working in the hearts of these women!

Now these women learned to work together, but they said, "We really do need a leader. Not just for us, but for the whole program." When the group talked about this, they decided this would be a good job for a vice president. They encouraged _____ to take on this task, and of course she said yes.

By now a sort of superstructure was being raised. Programs and coordinators, members, and committees; and they discovered that there was a lot of paperwork. "Hey," one of them said, "let's nominate a secretary. She can do the work of keeping minutes and a record of everything we do." The others thought that was a good idea, and they asked _____ to be the secretary. She smiled and said, "Of course I will!"

Something else came up. "What about money? If we're in mission, members are going to be sending in pledges. We need a treasurer." _____ was tapped for that job. "Well," the women said one day, "how are we doing? Do we need anyone else?" One woman spoke up: "Since we are nominating officers, we should include the pastor and *his* spouse. According to our bylaws, *she* is a member of the Executive Board, so let's name *her* honorary president." "That should do it" they said. However, one of the members said, "Hold it! Hold it! We're not quite finished. We have forgotten about a *leader!* Someone to tie it all together, to convene meetings, to represent us on the council and the administration board. We need a president."

They searched and thought and prayed. Then they asked _____ to be their president. She thought about it and prayed, and they all prayed again, and finally she said, "Yes, I will be your president."

Dear sisters, you are called together in a common purpose, to know God and to experience freedom as whole persons through Jesus Christ; to develop a creative, supportive fellowship, and to expand concepts of mission through participation in the global ministries of the church.

Response: Our purpose is all-encompassing. It is the tie that binds us, the concern that keeps us in mission, the very reason we exist in community. We seek to know God, to experience Jesus, to develop a supportive community, and to expand our knowledge of and participation in global ministry. This is what makes us function.

Pastor: I hold in my hand a ball of string, which is rather useless by itself. But when the ball is passed around the string can serve as a link between us. *(The string is passed to all, each holding a part of it, and so back to the pastor)*

Pastor: Each of you holds a special position, and your contribution will be unique. Still, it is all held together by your faith, and you are as one. *(Here the pastor may offer a few words based on the book of Ruth and/or I Corinthians, chapter 13)*

Pastor: I now hold one end of this ball of string that unites us all. I hold it as a symbol of unity and love. I dedicate each of us anew to the centrality of Christ, through whom we serve our God.

Response: We are linked together in a circle of love—love for our Lord and for each other.

Pastor: As we have looked back to the beginnings of this band of women, we have seen that the Lord was working in this place.

Response: We know it, and we thank him for it.

Pastor: Go in peace and in joy, knowing that the Lord will continue to work in you and through you.

Response: Amen.

INSTALLATION OF THE PRESIDENT AND OFFICERS OF AN ORGANIZATION IN THE CHURCH

(May be adapted to fit a particular organization)

Pastor: Welcome to all of you, our dear members and friends. We are here to worship our Lord and also to install into service the president and officers of the _____ society of this church. We ask for your prayers for them, your cooperation, and a showing of your love for them.

Paul wrote to the Philippians that he was thankful to God for the fellowship he enjoyed with the brothers and sisters in the faith.

People: We thank God for our fellowship, too.

Pastor: We have so much in common: we love the same Lord, we are redeemed by the same Lord, we all await his wonderful promises, and we will all be together forever in heaven with him.

People: Praise the Lord! *(The people may applaud in praise)*

Prayer: (Pastor and people pray together) Dear Lord, we are here today in this church to worship you and praise you and to install the president and officers of the _____ society. We pray for them and ask that you give them the needed devotion to service, and the courage and strength to do the tasks they must do.

President and Officers: Dear Lord, we are grateful for your presence here today. We ask your blessing on this service and we pray that the members of this congregation will support us and help us and show us by their love that they are happy to have us as their leaders.

(The pastor may give a message based on I John 1:3, II Corinthians 8:4, or Galatians 6:2)

THE INSTALLATION: *(President and officers come forward)*

Pastor: In the early days of the Church, the fellowship of Christians shared their love and sufferings and witnessing. They even shared their material possessions, redistributing them so that none in the fellowship would be in need. In a way, that is what we are doing today. You, _____, _____, and _____, have been blessed with certain talents of leadership and we, the people of this fellowship, have elected you to share these God-given talents with us so that no one in this fellowship will suffer from lack of leadership. We offer you our love and support and help. *(To the officers)* We are asking a great deal of you. Will you accept the responsibility?

Response: Yes, we gladly and prayerfully accept it.

Pastor: (To the congregation) Is it your wish that

these people serve as the president and officers of the _____ society?
Response: Yes, it most certainly is!
Pastor: Then, in the precious name of our Lord and Savior, I welcome you as the president and officers of the _____ society of this church. God go with you.
Response: Amen.

INSTALLATION OF THE OFFICERS OF A MEN'S ORGANIZATION

Pastor: Dear brothers and sisters in Christ: it has been said, and sometimes rightfully so, that the Church is composed of women and children. That it is the women who come to church and bring their children, and it is the women who do all the work. The men traditionally stay home on Sunday mornings and sleep or read the Sunday papers. However, in this church we can celebrate with a great deal of joy because we have a group of men who are eager to serve the Lord through his Church.
Congregation: Amen! And we do celebrate.
Pastor: This group has grown from a few devoted men to an active fellowship of _____ men who serve our church in many ways. And now they have elected officers to give them direction and purpose.
Congregation: We thank God for them.
Pastor: *(To the candidates)* Do you promise to serve this church through the men's organization?
Response: We promise to serve with love for our fellow members, and with a great deal of prayer, and with hard work whenever necessary.

Pastor: Will you keep in mind always that you represent the Christian Church and that other men are looking to you as an example?

Candidates: Yes, we are aware of that.

Pastor: Will you also be aware of the fact that you are not gathering together just for fellowship but also to look for ways in which you can further the gospel of Jesus Christ?

Candidates: Yes, we will search for ways to do that.

Pastor: (To the congregation) Will you, brothers and sisters in Christ, support these men with your love and your prayers; and will you respond with a willing yes when they ask for your help? Will you, our brothers, become an active part of this group? Will you, our sisters, encourage your husbands and brothers to join these men of God?

Response: Yes, we promise.

Pastor: In the light of these promises, I declare this group of men to be set apart in holy ministry, as the officers and leaders of the Men's Fellowship of this church. I promise that I, too, will join the congregation in loving support.

Response: Amen!

INSTALLATION OF THE OFFICERS
OF A YOUTH ORGANIZATION

Pastor: Men and women have stood before this altar and promised to serve this congregation in many and varied ways: as deacons and elders, as leaders and officers.

Congregation: And we thank God for them.

Pastor: I have stood before this altar, at my installation as your pastor, and promised to serve you with zeal and with love.

Congregation: And we thank God for you.

Pastor: However, we aren't the only ones who are willing and eager to serve the Lord in his Church. Our youth also want to serve him and you.

Congregation: We thank God for them, too.

Pastor: (To the candidates) Why do you want to serve in this church?

Candidates: Because our Lord has told us that he wants our love and our service.

Pastor: Do you promise with your whole hearts that you will work in the Youth Organization, doing everything you can to further its program?

Candidates: We promise.

Pastor: Will you turn often to the Word of God and to prayer for strength and wisdom?

Candidates: Yes, we will.

Pastor: Will you try your best to live lives that show a godly example to the youth of this church and of this community?

Candidates: Yes, we will try.

Pastor: (To the congregation) Dear brothers and sisters in Christ, will you accept these young people as the leaders of the Youth Organization of this congregation? Instead of brushing them aside with the words, "Oh, they're just kids," will you be aware of their desires and their potential, so that they will not be ashamed of their youth? Will you lift them up in prayer, recognizing the fact that they are the future leaders of Christ's Church on earth?

Congregation: Yes, we accept this as our sacred responsibility.

Pastor: Will you love them and help them whenever and wherever you can?

Congregation: Yes, we will love them and help them.

Pastor: *(To the candidates)* Dear young people, you have promised to act as mature, dedicated Christians as you serve the Lord through this organization, and the people of this church have promised to accept you as such. I now declare you the officers of the Youth Organization of _____ Church, and I ask for God's blessings on your efforts.

All: Amen.

INSTALLATION
OF A CHURCH SECRETARY

Pastor: *(To the congregation)* We are here today to receive and install _____ as the church secretary of the congregation.

(To the church secretary) _____, I know that you are a most capable secretary. I have seen evidence of your typing and business skills, and I know that you have had considerable office experience. However, the job of church secretary is so much more than an office job. You will not only be called upon to do an enormous amount of work yourself, but you will have to help others see their potential, help them work efficiently, and serve them with a servant's heart. Are you willing to work with the people of this congregation in that capacity?

Church Secretary: Yes, I am.

Pastor: You will be asked again and again to put

your own feelings and desires aside in order to please someone in this church. It will not be easy to try to please so many people, but it will be your task to try. Are you willing to do this?

Church Secretary: Yes, I am willing to try.

Pastor: As church secretary of this congregation, you will be expected to be a worker. It may not be glamorous or exciting, but you will be expected to accomplish what must be accomplished, day after day, so this congregation will run as smoothly as possible. Will you promise to do this?

Church Secretary: Yes, I promise.

Pastor: You will hear and know about confidential things in this congregation. It is absolutely essential that you be a keeper of secrets. Will you be?

Church Secretary: Yes, I most certainly will be.

Pastor: _____, the people of this congregation have hired you to serve as their church secretary. They will pay you a salary and they will try to support you in every possible way. They also want to love you and welcome you as a member of this church family. Will you accept that love and return it?

Church Secretary: Yes, I will be happy to do that.

Pastor: We see this as more than a job. We see it as a very special call from God. Typing, filing, running a mimeograph machine, and answering the phone may not seem like labors for the Lord, but they are. All of the work of the church office is done in the name of Jesus Christ and for the purpose of accomplishing what this congregation wants to accomplish, decently and in good order. You will represent this church of Jesus Christ through your daily work in the church office, and we trust you to represent us well. Do you accept this position of church secretary as a call from God to be his servant in the church office?

Church Secretary: Yes, I do believe that this is a call from God to serve him, and I accept that call with a willing heart.

Pastor: Members of this congregation, I ask you to accept _____ as our church secretary.

People: We accept *her* with loving hearts.

Pastor: I exhort you to treat *her* like a fellow worker in this church, not to expect the impossible from *her*, not to burden *her* with your problems and trials. I ask you to consider the pressure times and the busy days and to help lighten *her* load if you can. Work together to provide *her* with a decent office space, the best equipment we can afford, and a salary that matches what *she* does for us. Above all, remember *her* in your prayers.

People: We will do all of these things, with God's help.

Pastor: _____, this congregation welcomes you as their church secretary, and I welcome you as a member in team ministry. I pledge to you my support and my Christian love.

All: Amen.

CELEBRATING THE INSTALLATION OF A MISSION COMMITTEE

Pastor: I thank God that you are all here today to help in the installation of our Mission Committee. Have you come prepared to pray for them?

Response: Yes, we have.

Pastor: Have you come prepared to tell them what is expected of them?

Response: Yes, we have.

Pastor: Have you come prepared to help them, to stand behind them, to uplift them with your love and loyalty?

Response: Yes, we have.

Pastor: Then it is with a great deal of confidence that we begin this installation service.

People: Amen.

Pastor: (To the candidates) This congregation is asking a few people, _____, _____, and _____, to do a very big job. We are asking you to serve as our Mission Committee, and that means that we will be expecting you to bring the good news of Jesus Christ to as many people as you possibly can. It means that we will be hoping and praying that you will bring people to this church. It also means that we want you to seize every opportunity to spread the word about Jesus Christ to people far away, to people confined to institutions, in prisons, in other neighborhoods, other worlds. Yes, it is a very big job, and one of the most important tasks we Christians have to do. We are grateful to you for accepting the call to service, and we want to help. Let me remind you that you don't have to tackle this big job without any tools. There are some available, and it is my prayer that you will use them.

There is the Word of God: this book will serve as your handbook, and it will assure you over and over that the Lord wants us to be fishers of men. Also, God will tell you where to go to find the souls who need him. Rely on his wisdom. Peter fished and caught no fish and didn't know why. After the Lord told him where to drop his net, he caught many fish.

You also have the tool of patience. Develop it and nurture it and learn to wait on the Lord.

Finally, experience joy in what you are doing. There is no greater joy than in bringing a soul to Jesus Christ.

I now ask the members of this congregation if they will promise to pray every day for the members of this committee.

Response: Yes, we will pray for them.

Pastor: I ask you also if you will be supportive and will help them when they ask you to.

Response: Yes, we will help them whenever and however we can.

Pastor: Members of the Mission Committee: in view of the promised prayers and support of the members of this congregation, are you willing to serve as our Mission Committee?

Response: Yes, we are.

Pastor: We welcome you and we thank God for you.

Response: Amen.

LITANY OF DEDICATION
FOR HIGH SCHOOL GRADUATES

In some churches, special attention is paid each year to the High School graduates in the congregation. The graduates are honored at breakfasts, dinners, meetings in the church or parsonage, and mention of them is made at worship services. Graduation is celebrated at proms and at home parties, and it is important that the church also honor them, celebrate with them, and send them on their way with God's blessing. This litany could be used during a Sunday morning worship service. The leader could be the pastor or a number of people in the congregation.

Leader: To the end that every growing experience of the days of your youth may be an expression of God's will being done on earth; to the end that your friends, homes, schools, church, and nation may be touched by his hand working through you:

Youth: We dedicate ourselves to the principles and ideals of Jesus Christ.

Leader: That the marvelous energy that quickens the muscles and nerves of your bodies may move to the defense of all that is right and good; that the skill and work of your hands may create new beauty and usefulness for many:

Youth: We dedicate our physical selves, with their sensations of strength, weariness, pleasure, and pain, to God's work among his people.

Leader: In the hope that your searching and study will reveal more of God and give you insights for the betterment of many; with the conviction that the contemplation of the past and present will guide you in making decisions in accordance with God's will; in the hope that you will want to exercise your reason so that prejudices and ignorance may vanish; so that your imaginations may form plans for yourselves, your home, and your community on the foundations of God:

Youth: We give over to God our minds, with their powers of thinking, studying, and planning.

Leader: So that your sweeping emotions, which carry you to love and hate alike, may bring you only to a sincere love of all people; so that your binding friendships may unite young lives in a spirit of sharing; that you may aspire to the higher goals of life; that your hearts may be filled with compassion for the oppressed of the world, moving your hands to acts of love and service to them:

Youth: We dedicate our emotions, with their compassion and anger, distress and happiness, to God's eternal and universal love and mercy.

Leader: To the end that you may search after the purpose of life as a standard by which all else may be judged; that you will desire greatly to commune with God in order to know his will for you and for everyone; that you may pray that the Spirit of Jesus Christ will pervade your spirits:

Youth: We give to God our spiritual selves, which can be fed only by his Spirit, and strengthened only as we come to him.

Leader: That your hands may be his hands, that your thoughts may be of whatever is true, honorable, just, pure, lovely, excellent, and worthy of praise; knowing that the greatest of all things is love, and that you must worship God in spirit and in truth:

Youth: We hereby dedicate ourselves in obedience to the commandments of Jesus Christ: "You shall love the Lord your God with all your heart, and with all your soul, and with all your mind. . . . You shall love your neighbor as yourself."

Leader (or minister): Lord, look at us! Look at these young people! Today, they have dedicated themselves to you, and we believe them and love them and lift them up to you. In every age since the beginning of time, people have criticized their youth and held little hope for them; but Lord, look at these young people! They are different, they are set apart, because of their love for you. You alone, Lord, have

made all the difference, and we praise you. Be with
our young people as they go on to higher education,
to work, to whatever path they choose. They are
dedicated to serving you, Lord, and we ask for your
continued presence in their lives.

All: God go with you and put everlasting joy and
peace in your hearts. Amen.

LITANY
FOR A LEAVETAKING

*The following is not an Installation Service, but
rather a litany of love for members of the church who
are leaving that body and going to another city or
location. (Or perhaps college students who are
leaving.) This can be incorporated into a regular
worship service or be a part of a special service. If it is
used in a regular service, perhaps there will be a
coffee hour afterward, in which everyone will have an
opportunity to bid them goodbye; or it may be used at
a special dinner meeting held just for those who are
leaving. Maybe at a picnic or barbecue the litany can
be repeated over a fire.*

*In today's mobile society, every congregation
experiences these comings and goings, and it might
be a very good idea to take special note of them.*

Leader: Dear Lord, we are here today to say
goodbye to _____ and _____.

Response: And we are here to praise and worship
you, Lord.

Leader: We give thanks for the presence of these
brothers and sisters among us.

Response: For the time that we have had them with us.

Leader: And now they have to travel to another place and minister among other people.

Response: We will miss them!

Leader: Oh yes, Lord, we will miss them, but we know that you will bless them on their way and that you will be with them wherever they are.

Response: That is our deep and sincere prayer.

Leader: We pray that the close ties of love that we have had will not be broken by this separation.

Response: We will keep them close in our hearts and memories.

Leader: Lead them to another house of worship, Lord, where they may continue to serve you.

Response: To another group of brothers and sisters in Christ, where they may experience love and joy.

Leader: Lead them to further service in your Kingdom here on earth.

Response: To more love for thee.

Leader: _____ and _____, we will miss you. You have served the Lord and his church well, and we thank God for you. We don't want you to leave us, but we pray that you go in peace, that you go to serve the Lord, and that you will remember us in your hearts.

Congregation: Amen.